T0029101

To:

_____

From:

_____

Date:

_____

Love You, Little Lady

BRETT YOUNG

AIRIN O'CALLAGHAN

Tommy NELSON®

An Imprint of Thomas Nelson

Love You, Little Lady

© 2021 Brett Young

Tommy Nelson, PO Box 141000, Nashville, TN 37214

All rights reserved. No portion of this book may be reproduced, stored in a retrieval system, or transmitted in any form or by any means—electronic, mechanical, photocopy, recording, scanning, or other—except for brief quotations in critical reviews or articles, without the prior written permission of the publisher.

Published in Nashville, Tennessee, by Tommy Nelson. Tommy Nelson is an imprint of Thomas Nelson. Thomas Nelson is a registered trademark of HarperCollins Christian Publishing, Inc.

Tommy Nelson titles may be purchased in bulk for educational, business, fund-raising, or sales promotional use. For information, please email SpecialMarkets@ThomasNelson.com.

ISBN 978-1-4002-2503-3 (eBook)
ISBN 978-1-4002-2507-1 (HC)

Library of Congress Cataloging-in-Publication Data

Names: Young, Brett, 1981- author. | O'Callaghan, Airin, illustrator.
Title: Love you, little lady / Brett Young; illustrated by Airin O'Callaghan.
Description: Nashville: Thomas Nelson, 2021. | Audience: Ages 4–8 | Summary: "From country music sensation Brett Young comes a heartwarming celebration of parental love and tenderness based on his touching song "Lady.""—Provided by publisher.
Identifiers: LCCN 2020056010 (print) | LCCN 2020056011 (ebook) | ISBN 9781400225071 (hardcover) | ISBN 9781400225033 (epub)
Subjects: LCSH: Young, Brett, 1981–Juvenile literature. | Fathers and daughters—Juvenile literature. | Mothers and daughters—Juvenile literature.
Classification: LCC ML3930.Y67 Y68 2021 (print) | LCC ML3930.Y67 (ebook) | DDC 782.421642092 [B]—dc23
LC record available at https://lccn.loc.gov/2020056010
LC ebook record available at https://lccn.loc.gov/2020056011

Written by Brett Young with Jean Fischer
Illustrated by Airin O'Callaghan

Printed in South Korea

21 22 23 24 25 SAM 6 5 4 3 2 1

Mfr: SAM / Seoul, South Korea / July 2021 / PO #12040401

To my beautiful girls,
Taylor, Presley, and baby girl Young, who is on the way.

And to our incredible mothers
and all the wonderful mothers out there
who continue to set examples for their children
with their actions every day.

The **moment** I first heard your heart,
I wondered how I'd do.

I'd never been a dad before,
but your mama **helped me through**.

We **welcomed** you into the world,
holding you nice and tight.
We counted toes
and kissed your nose
and **kept you close** all night.

First you cried and

then you cooed.

These turned to **giggles** and **words**.

Of all the music
in the world,
it's the
sweetest sound
we've heard!

You wobbled toward my outstretched arms.
Mom led you **foot by foot**.

And now you've figured out each step,
baby girl, you won't stay put!

You can always run to Daddy.

You'll forever be my baby.

I'll **hold** and **hug** you

in my arms.

I LOVE YOU, LITTLE LADY.

You are so much like your mama.
**You're sweet
and kind
and smart.**
When you do good things for others,
it comes straight from your heart.

When you and Mom play dress-up

and pretend to **save the world**,

I'm proud to be the daddy

of the **bravest** little girl!

I'll try to teach a thing or two,
like to face life with a **smile**.

Remember that some things you do
are hard and **take a while**.

When we learn new things **together**,
just watch your mom because
you'll see close to **perfect patience**
in everything she does.

You can always run to Daddy.
You'll forever be **my baby**.
But look at Mama, baby girl,
and you'll learn to **be a lady**.

I hope you'll be a lot like Mom—
calm and kind and caring.
And maybe you'll be a bit like me—
adventurous and **daring**.

You'll **always** be a bit like us

in everything you do.

But as you **stretch your wings** to fly,

you'll learn to be like *you!*

You're **growing up**, baby girl.
Who knows what life may bring?
As you explore this **stunning** world,
remember this one thing . . .

You can always run to Mom and me.
You'll forever be **our baby**.
In all you do, we'll help you through.

WE LOVE YOU, LITTLE LADY.